Allegro molto moderato
Flauti
Oboi
Clarinetti in A
Fagotti
pp
a 2
Corni in E
Trombe in C
3 Tromboni
pp Tuba
Timpani in E
pp
loco
Allegro molto moderato
Solo
Piano forte
ff
(Tutti)
Allegro molto moderato
Violini
pizz
p
pizz
p
Viola
pizz

# N O R W A Y

## Svalbard

Nordaustlandet
Spitsbergen
Barentsøya
Edgeøya
Longyearbyen

## Facts about Norway

*System of government:*
Constitutional monarchy

*Area:*
386,958 square kilometres,
including Svalbard and
Jan Mayen.

*Total length of coastline:*
21,340 kilometres, including
fjords.

*Borders with other countries:*
With Russia:
196 kilometres
With Finland
727 kilometres
With Sweden
1,619 kilometres

*Currency unit:*
Norwegian kroner (NOK)

*Largest lake:*
Lake Mjøsa, 368 square
kilometres

*Longest river:*
Glomma, 598 kilometres

*Highest mountain:*
Galdhøpiggen, 2,469 metres

*Population:*
Approx. 4,370,000

## The ten largest towns

| | Pop. approx.: |
|---|---|
| Oslo (1) | 487,000 |
| Bergen (2) | 223,000 |
| Trondheim (3) | 143,000 |
| Stavanger (4) | 104,000 |
| Kristiansand (5) | 69,000 |
| Fredrikstad (6) | 65,000 |
| Tromsø (7) | 56,000 |
| Drammen (8) | 53,000 |
| Skien (9) | 49,000 |
| Sandnes (10) | 48,000 |

# Contents

# This is Norway

*The old trading post on Kjerringøy.*

# AT THE TOP OF EUROPE

*Norway is situated far north on the world map, right at the top of Europe. A large proportion of the country lies north of the Arctic Circle. Even Norway's name means "The way to the North". Today, Norway is a well-developed democracy, a modern industrial nation and an active member of the world community.*

## AT THE TOP OF EUROPE

Norway borders on Russia, Finland and Sweden to the east and the Atlantic Ocean to the west. If you include the fjords, the coastline is more than 20,000 kilometres long. The distance in a direct line from the southernmost point (Lindesnes) to the northernmost tip (North Cape) is 1,750 kilometres. Most of the population lives in the south and population density is highest around Oslo, the capital city. Thanks to the Gulf Stream, the warm current that originates in the Gulf of Mexico, it is possible to live at latitudes which in other parts of the world are populated only by indigenous peoples.

The Svalbard archipelago and the islands of Bjørnøya and Jan Mayen are Norwegian sovereign territory. Peter I Island and Bouvet Island in the Antarctic are also under Norwegian supremacy.

## Dramatic landscape

There are great variations in Norway, summer or winter. If you travel inland from the mild coastal climate, you will soon reach mountainous regions where the weather conditions are considerably more extreme. The coastline is broken by narrow fjords which reach up to 200 kilometres inland. The fjords and the surrounding mountains, which rise steeply from the water to a height of over a thousand metres, are among Norway's most popular tourist attractions. The landscape in Eastern and Central Norway is less dramatic.

Northern Norway is beautiful, rugged and weather-beaten. In

summer it is light all night thanks to the midnight sun. In winter it is always dark, with just a glimpse of light at midday. The Norwegians make active use of their beautiful surroundings. Many of them are members of sports clubs devoted to a variety of outdoor activities. Everyone has the right to walk or ski on uncultivated land without the permission of the landowner. Property has traditionally been fairly equally distributed, and Norway is still a relatively egalitarian, homogeneous society. Almost 90 per cent of the population belong the state Lutheran church, the vast majority are educated at state schools, and until the 1980s there was only one channel each for radio and television. Due to all these factors, the Norwegians have a common value base and a relatively uniform approach to political and social issues, regardless of where they live. Nevertheless, the different regions have their own cultural characteristics and a diversity of dialects, illustrated by the fact

that Norway has two official written languages in addition to the language of the indigenous Sami population in the North.

## Trains, ferries and planes

Norway is a long, narrow country. Due to the mountains and fjords, constructing and maintaining roads and railways is an expensive, complicated process. Along the coast, ferries are often the only means of getting from one place to another, although they are increasingly being replaced by bridges and tunnels. While it is possible to go by train from Stavanger in the south to Bodø

*The Flåm valley and the Flåm railway.*

in the north, the main way of travelling from one part of the country to the other is by air. Large aircraft fly to the largest towns, Svalbard and international destinations while smaller planes service regular routes to an extensive network of short runway airports in the less accessible regions.

*The Okstind glacier facing Tvillingtinden.*

*Stortinget – the national assembly.*

*The 1814 Constitution.*

## A Modern Society

Modern Norway is a well-established democracy with comprehensive welfare services and free education for all.

### Freedom and democracy

Norway is a constitutional monarchy. Although the King has no real political power, the Royal Family is loved and respected by the Norwegian people. Legislative power lies with the national assembly, the Storting, for which elections are held every four years. Relations between the Storting and the Government are based on a parliamentary system, which means that the Government must have the support of a majority of the 165 members of the Storting. Representatives are also elected to the Sameting, the highest popularly elected body of the Sami people. Local government elections are held every fourth year.

The rich flora of special interest organisations provides another channel for the democratic process. On the basis of long-established practice, the authorities consult all relevant organisations when important legislation is being prepared. Norway also has several *ombudsmen* to whom citizens may apply if their appeals to other authorities are unsuccessful. They include the Ombudsman for Public Administration, the Consumer Ombudsman and the Gender Equality Ombud. Norway also has a Commissioner for Children to safeguard children's interests. The press is often called "the fourth estate". The Norwegians are among the keenest newspaper readers in the world and have nearly 150 different newspapers to choose between.

### Women in power

Norway has made active efforts to increase the proportion of women in politics and public administration. Thanks to these efforts, Norway has more women in public office than most other countries. The proportion of women in the cabinet and the national assembly has been high since the mid-1980s. The largest political parties have all had women leaders and many senior civil servants are women. Norway's first woman bishop was appointed in 1993.

### Security and welfare

Norway was one of the first countries to develop a modern welfare state based on a financial safety net that is intended to provide social and economic security for all.

Statue of King Karl Johan in front of the Royal Palace in Oslo.

own Constitution. The Swedish king accepted the Constitution with certain amendments, which resulted in a personal union that was finally dissolved in 1905.

The Royal Family: King Harald, Queen Sonja, Crown Prince Haakon Magnus and Princess Märtha Louise.

All citizens are members of national insurance and pension schemes which cover medical treatment, old-age pensions, disability pensions and a wide range of welfare services. In recent years, there has been considerable emphasis on improving the situation for families with small children. In addition to child benefits for all families, generous, flexible parental leave schemes have been introduced for both parents in connection with pregnancy and birth.

Over 90 per cent of children attend state schools, where tuition is free of charge. School is compulsory for the first nine years and everyone is legally entitled to upper secondary education.

## From the Ice Age to the present day

The first humans settled in Norway after the end of the Ice Age, about 10,000 years ago. For many thousands of years, people lived from hunting, fishing and farming. The first Viking raids and expeditions to other countries took place at the end of the 8th century. King Harald Hairfair united Norway around AD 900 and at the height of the Middle Ages, the Kingdom of Norway also included several islands in the west, including the Faeroes, Iceland, Greenland and parts of the British Isles.

Norway entered into union with Denmark in 1380 and officially became a Danish province in 1537. In 1814, Norway was ceded to the King of Sweden in the wake of the Napoleonic Wars. In the same year, the Norwegians declared their independence and adopted their

## Water, oil and gas

Modern industry in Norway was originally based on hydro-electric power, and all electricity supplies for industry and households still come from this renewable, non-polluting energy source.

Oil and gas have been produced on the Norwegian continental shelf since the 1970s and Norway is currently Europe's biggest oil exporter and one of the main suppliers of gas to the European continent. Oil and gas production have strongly influenced the development of Norwegian industry and have also provided considerable revenues for the state in the form of taxes and royalties.

## Industry and shipping

Norway is a major producer of aluminium, ferrosilicon and magnesium and has a petrochemical industry based on North Sea oil and gas. Norway is also one of the world's largest producers of artificial fertilizer. Nevertheless, the majority of Norwegian companies are small or medium-sized. Pharmaceuticals, electronics, services, fish processing and traditional shipbuilding are all important sectors. Norway's shipyards have specialised in building advanced vessels designed for special purposes. Norway is also a major supplier of equipment and services for the world's shipping fleet and is currently the fourth largest shipping nation in the world.

## Fishing, agriculture and forestry

Fishing has been one of Norway's most important export industries ever since the Middle Ages. Today, in addition to the fish that is caught on the fishing grounds, large quantities of fish come from the aquaculture industry, and salmon from Norwegian fish farms is sold all over the world.

## TOWARDS THE NEXT MILLENNIUM

Much of Norway's industry is based on utilising the country's rich natural resources. Nevertheless, few countries are more dependent upon foreign trade. In order to meet the challenges of the future, private companies and public authorities are investing considerable resources in research and development.

*Oil rigs in the North Sea.*

Only 3.5 per cent of Norway's land mass consists of arable land. Norwegian farmers nevertheless supply most of the country's food requirements. Although Norwegian agricultural products are exported to only a limited extent, the forests provide important exports in the form of timber, paper, paperboard, cellulose, building materials and furniture. The primary industries are extremely important since they provide employment and maintain population patterns in the outlying regions.

*Roald Amundsen reached the South Pole on 14 December 1911.*

# EXCEEDING THE LIMITS

All countries have people who have achieved something special, men and women who have dared to go a step further than others. The Norwegian men and women mentioned here have one thing in common – their names have become famous all over the world.

## The adventurers

When Norwegian *Roald Amundsen* (1872–1928) returned from the South Pole, he was celebrated as the first person to have reached this central point in the icy Antarctic wastes. He was also the first person to sail through the North-West Passage, north of Canada. *Fridtjof Nansen* (1861–1930) led a many-faceted life as a scientist, polar explorer, artist and politi-

cian. He crossed Greenland on skis and the North Polar Sea on the "Fram". Nansen was awarded the Nobel Peace Prize in 1922 for his efforts to repatriate refugees after the First World War and for his work on behalf of the starving population of the former Soviet Union. Scientist *Thor Heyerdahl* (1914–) is one of the best known explorers of our time. On the raft "Kon-Tiki", he sailed from South America to Polynesia to prove that the Indians could have undertaken this journey many centuries before. In the same way, on the papyrus boat "Ra", he demonstrated that man could have crossed the Atlantic in ancient times.

*Fridtjof Nansen*

*Thor Heyerdahl*

## Ice skates and running shoes

Sonja Henie (1912–69) won ten world ice skating championships and was Olympic champion three times. In the USA she became a film star and toured with her own ice show. She founded the Henie-Onstad Art Museum at Høvikodden, just outside Oslo.

Few Norwegian women know New York's asphalt better than *Grete Waitz* (1953–). She has won the New York and London marathons, the world marathon and the world cross country title. Grete Waitz will be remembered for breaking barriers in the field of women's long-distance running.

*Sonja Henie*

## Peaceful competition

Sport is the largest mass movement in Norway. It also brings people from many countries together in peaceful competition. Norway has arranged many major events. The Olympic Winter Games were first held in Oslo in 1952, and were again hosted by Norway in 1994, this time at Lillehammer. The Norwegian public appreciates good sporting achievements. At the Lillehammer Olympics, they cheered as loudly for the sportsmen and women of other nations as they did for Norway's own heroes, and many observers maintained that the public were the real winners.

*Kindest regards*
*Sonja Henie*

*Henrik Ibsen*

## Writers and painters

Norway has a rich cultural life and has produced many artists of high international standing. Some of those who have already won their place in history and serve as sources of inspiration for contemporary authors and artists are presented below.

Of course you can see "Ghosts" and "A Doll's House" by *Henrik Ibsen* (1828–1906) at a Norwegian theatre. But you are just as likely to see Ibsen's plays in New York, London, Paris or Berlin. Ibsen brought a psychological depth and social relevance to European theatre that had not been seen since Shakespeare's time.

Three Norwegian authors have been awarded the Nobel Prize for Literature. *Bjørnstjerne Bjørnson* (1832–1910) won the prize in 1903. He wrote short stories, novels, poems and plays. He also wrote the text of the Norwegian national anthem. When *Knut Hamsun* (1859–1952) won the Nobel Prize in 1920 for his book *Markens Grøde* (Growth of the Soil) he had already written many other major works, including "Hunger", "Pan" and "Victoria".

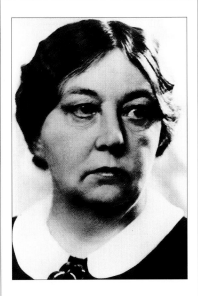

*Bjørnstjerne Bjørnson*

*"The Scream", painted by Edvard Munch in 1893.*

*Sigrid Undset*

*Sigrid Undset* (1882–1949) was awarded the prize in 1928. Her best known work is the trilogy "Kristin Lavransdatter", which has been translated into many languages and has recently been made into a film.

*Knut Hamsun*

Few paintings awaken such recognition as "The Scream" by *Edvard Munch* (1863–1944). He portrayed loneliness, anxiety and death, but also love, joy and life. Munch was one of the forerunners of the expressionist movement. Composer *Edvard Grieg* (1843–1907) is perhaps best known for "Morning" from the first of the two "Peer Gynt" suites. Here, as in many other of his works, Grieg uses the sounds and harmonies of Norwegian folk music. His A minor concerto is on the repertoire of many famous pianists.

# The Oslo Fjord

# OSLO – CAPITAL CITY IN AN IDYLLIC SETTING

*Oslo is a modern European city with an exciting history and an interesting cultural life. And no other major city offers the same opportunities for experiencing the joys of nature, for Oslo is surrounded by sea and forests on all sides. In contrast, the night life is hectic and exciting. Oslo has something for everyone.*

## The Viking town

Oslo was founded by the Vikings and became the country's capital under Harald Hardråde in the mid-11th century. Unfortunately many of the old buildings were des-troyed in the great fire of 1624, but the town was rebuilt in the same year by Danish King Christian IV and named Christiania. Three hundred years later, the city was renamed Oslo after Norway became independent in 1905.

*Gustav Vigeland's sculpture "Sinnataggen" (The Angry Child) in the Vigeland Park.*

## A city of holidays and festivals

Oslo is a mixture of stock exchange and beaches, business and pleasure. Within a radius of a couple of kilometres you will find the Royal Palace, Huk beach, Akershus Castle, the Holmenkollen ski jump, the parliament building and the never-resting Aker Brygge dockland complex with shops, cinemas, restaurants and a marina.

In these beautiful surroundings, Oslo lives a hectic summer life with jazz and chamber music festivals, a children's carnival, a rock festival at Kalvøya and a summer concert at Holmenkollen.

## White-painted idyll

A short car journey from Oslo along the east coast of the fjord lie the white-painted towns of Drøbak and Son, full of

## Nature and culture

Norwegians are fond of the outdoor life and in Oslo a sail on the fjord, a walk in the woods around Lake Sogn or a ski in the forest are always within easy reach.
So are Edvard Munch's paintings at the Munch Museum, Norwegian and European art exhibitions at the Henie-Onstad Museum, an Ibsen performance at the National Theatre, sculptures at the Vigeland Park and rural Bygdøy with the Viking ships, the Folk Museum, Fridtjof Nansen's polar vessel "Fram" and Thor Heyerdahl's balsa wood raft, "Kon Tiki".

boats and bathers. And on the west side of the fjord lie Edvard Munch's Åsgårdstrand and the trading town of Tønsberg, one of Norway's oldest settlements, with lively summer activities and beautiful beaches at Nøtterøy and fashionable Tjøme.

*Outdoor restaurant by the National Theatre.*

*Oslo is surrounded by forests, used by the townspeople for recreation, summer and winter.*

*Statue of King Olav by the Holmenkollen ski jump.*

# THE VIGELAND PARK

*The Vigeland Park is one of Norway's most popular tourist attractions.*

The park contains 212 sculptures in bronze, granite and wrought iron by Gustav Vigeland (1869–1943). Most of them stand along an 850 metre-long axis and depict people of all ages, from birth to death. With the adjacent Frogner Park, the sculpture park is the largest, most beautiful park in Oslo. It functions both as a place of recreation and a magnet for tourists. Almost two million people a year find their way here in the course of a year. The monolith plateau, the highest point of the sculpture park, is where Vigeland placed his seventeen-metre-high column of human bodies – called the Monolith because it is sculpted from one block of stone.

In few other places in the world is a nation's love of its native country expressed in such generous, festive celebration as Norway's Constitution Day. There are no military parades, although 17 May also marks independence from centuries of union with Denmark and Sweden.

### Banners and flags, buns and fizzy pop

Constitution Day starts in the morning with a salute of cannon and the playing of the national anthem by thousands of school bands in towns and villages, fjords and mountains all over the country. Families and friends meet for breakfast before the children's procession begins, and for the youngsters the day is one long succession of buns, cakes, ice cream and fizzy pop. They march in the procession in their finest clothes, each waving a Norwegian flag and wearing ribbons in the Norwegian colours. Every

procession is headed by the school brass band and the teachers carrying flags and banners.

### In honour of the Royal Family

The 17th May celebrations in Oslo are always rather special because the children's procession with its thousands of singing children marches up main street, Karl Johan, past the Storting and finally defiles past the Royal Palace. The Royal Family stands on the balcony and waves for as long as the procession lasts. There is plenty of national symbolism in this

# CONSTITUTION DAY – NORWAY IN RED, WHITE AND BLUE

*May is the month when spring comes to Norway, so Constitution Day is a joyful celebration, full of hope and promise. This national holiday is primarily intended to celebrate the memory of the men who wrote Norway's Constitution, which was signed at Eidsvoll on 17 May 1814. But Constitution Day has also become a day for children, a day of brass bands and national costumes.*

joyful meeting between people and monarch. But throughout history 17 May has also been a day for campaigning, officials against farmers (1870–80), workers against the bourgeoisie (1920–30), Norwegians against Germans during the occupation (1940–45) and for and against Norwegian membership of the European Union (1972 and 1994).

## The Norwegian national anthem

Ja, vi elsker dette landet
som det stiger frem
furet, værbitt over vannet
med de tusen hjem.
Elsker, elsker det og tenker
på vår far og mor
:/: og den saganatt som senker
drømme på vår jord. :/:

*The first verse of the Norwegian national anthem*

# EDVARD MUNCH

*"In my art I have tried to find out about life and the meaning of life. I have also tried to help others to understand life," wrote Edvard Munch. He lived a restless, turbulent existence characterised by long sojourns in Berlin and Paris, unhappy love affairs, periods in sanatoria and, in the final years, withdrawn isolation at his home, Ekely, in Oslo. Edvard Munch was born in 1863 and died in 1944.*

## A sensitive child

The man who was a forerunner of expressionism in Germany and the Nordic countries grew up in Christiania, which was the name of Norway's capital until 1924. He was the son of a military doctor at Akershus Castle, a deeply religious man who lost his wife in 1868 and was left to bring up five small children. Edvard's older sister, Johanne Sophie, died of tuberculosis nine years later.

Edvard Munch himself was often ill during childhood and was away from school for long periods of time. As a mature painter, his art was influenced by his memories of illness, death and grief. However, the motifs in his first drawings and water colours are from his home environment; interiors and small, everyday things such as a medicine bottle, a toothbrush and the view from the windows in the apartment where he spent so much time as a child.

*The Dance of Life 1899–1900*

## Breaking with convention

On Monday 8 November 1880, 17-year-old Munch wrote in his diary "I have once again left the technical school. I have now decided to become a painter." His father was distressed. He feared the unfortunate influence of artistic circles and the unpromising economic prospects his son's choice entailed. In the 1880s, the young painter took part in the World Exhibition in Antwerp, travelled to Paris and saw the collection of paintings at the Louvre and the annual exhibition of contemporary art at the Salon, and made friends with the infamous, dissolute writer Hans Jæger, who was leader of the "Christiania Bohemians". Munch's participation in the Autumn Exhibition in 1886 with the painting "The Sick Child" was a turning point in his career. The critics were highly scathing of his painting, which is based on scenes from his sister Johanne Sophie's death. However, recognition came a few years later in the form of a state grant and Munch returned to Paris. Influenced by the ideas of Hans Jæger and the Bohemians about "writing your life", Edvard Munch began to note down his memories of childhood and adolescence and his "spiritual experiences". Love and anxiety soon became opposite poles in Munch's paintings. He wanted to paint "living people who breathe, feel, suffer and love". That was what the painting of tomorrow should be concerned with.

## "Scandal" and honour in Berlin

In Paris, Munch became a pupil of Léon Bonnat and gained important impulses from the city's artists, who were finding new ways out of naturalism and realism.

In 1892, Munch exhibited his paintings at the Berlin Art Society. They were savaged by the critics, who believed the entire exhibition to be "an insult to art". However, in the 1890s Munch became a well-known personality in Berlin's artistic circles. He rented a studio and experienced an inspired period, producing the motifs for "The Frieze of Life", a cycle on the themes of love, anxiety and death, and painting "Vampire", "Madonna" and "Death in the Sick Room", the latter yet another motif from his traumatic experiences in connection with his sister's death in 1877. In the wine bar "Zum Schwartzen Ferkel", he met like-minded German and Scandinavian artists and made friends with Swedish author August Strindberg, Polish poet Stanislaw Przybyszewski and Norwegian sculptor Gustav Vigeland.

## Europe and Åsgårdstrand

During the years of exhibitions and long sojourns in Berlin and Paris, Edvard Munch bought a house in the small town of Åsgård-strand, about 150 kilometres south of Christiania, where he had spent many summers as a child. Much of the landscape, the town and the beaches can be seen in Munch's paintings. Today, the house and the studio are a museum. "Walking in Åsgårdstrand is like walking among my paintings," he said on one occasion. During this period, he had an affair with a rich merchant's daughter from Christiania who also frequented Bohemian circles. The relation-ship came to a dramatic end in summer 1902 with a shooting incident at Åsgårdstrand where Munch was wounded in the left hand. This led to a breach with his Bohemian friends in Christi-ania and affected Edvard Munch for many years after-wards. In the same year, he made his final breakthrough in Germany and on the continent, ten years after the "scandalous" exhibition at the Berlin Art Society. Munch became acquainted with Dr. Max Linde in Lübeck, his first important patron. Dr. Linde had recently written an enthusiastic publica-tion entitled "Edvard Munch und die Kunst der Zukunft".

## Recognition and nervous breakdown

The years that followed were extremely hectic and productive, with exhibitions and commissions for portraits of prominent people. "Dr. Linde's sons" (1904) is an example of brilliant portraiture and represents a change in Munch's choice of motif.

Edvard Munch was also a brilliant graphic artist. His first woodcuts were produced in cooperation with the famous printer Auguste Clot. Today, Edvard Munch is regarded as one of the classic graphic artists. Nevertheless, nervous exhaus-tion, an irregular lifestyle and heavy drinking had taken their toll. During the period 1905–07, he was admitted to various sanatoria in Germany. The painting "Self portrait with wine bottle" is from this period. In 1907, he painted "Bathing men" on the beach at Wärne-münde, a celebration of vital masculinity. But he still had

*«Madonna» 1893/94.*

38

*«Kiss» 1897.*

*Edvard Munch's house in Åsgårdstrand.*

problems with his health. Due to alcoholic excess, hallucinations and a persecution complex he was forced to spend eight months at a clinic in Copenhagen.

## At home at Ekely

Edvard Munch's journey back to his home town of Christiania took place in stages. For many years, he lived and painted in other parts of Norway, at Kragerø, Hvitsten and Jeløya, just outside Moss. This is where he found the motifs for the large murals in the University of Oslo Aula.

In 1913, he and Pablo Picasso were the only foreigners invited to have their own room at the Autumn Exhibition in Berlin. In 1916, Munch purchased a large property called Ekely at Skøyen, just outside Oslo. He lived and worked there until his death, seeing only his family, a few friends and his animals (he jokingly called himself a "gentleman farmer"). He now only made short trips abroad –

to Berlin, Paris, Zürich and other European cities. On his seventieth birthday in 1933, he was honoured with the Grand Cross of the Order of St. Olav. Edvard Munch died of pneumonia on 23 January 1944. In his will, he left all his paintings to the City of Oslo.

*Edvard Munch at Ekely.*

# Southern Norway

# THE SOUTH COAST AND TELEMARK

*The coast from Kragerø to Lindesnes in southern Norway is an idyllic place for summer holidays. It is a region of boats, warm rocks and white-painted villages. Here you can enjoy a sailing holiday and relax to the sound of seagulls over a myriad small islands, or eat at a fish restaurant in an old sailmaker's workshop on the quayside.*

Thanks to centuries of shipping, fishing and trading traditions, small towns and villages have grown up all along the coast of southern Norway. Risør, Grimstad and Lillesand are just three of the beautiful harbour towns where people come all summer long to experience wooden boat festivals, cultural events and the relaxed holiday atmosphere. Lindesnes lies at the southernmost tip of Norway. From here it is 2,518 kilometres to North Cape, the northernmost point. Kristiansand, the largest town in southern Norway, was founded by King Christian IV in 1641 and is a communications link for traffic to and from the continent. *Risør.*

*A sailing ship enters the harbour
– perhaps to repair a sail or to buy provisions.*

## Trout fishing, rural culture and Telemark skiing

In the inland mountains, lakes lie waiting to tempt the trout fisherman and in Setesdal folk music and the traditional arts of the silversmith are still very much alive. The mountain resort of Hovden is here too. Morgedal in Telemark is known as the cradle of skiing. This was the home of Sondre Norheim, the founder of modern ski sports.

Close by is one of the most popular tourist attractions in the area, the Kristiansand Zoo, which offers a variety of activities for the whole family. A trip on the Setesdal Railway on a veteran train from 1869 is another unforgettable experience. You can also travel far into the mountains on one of the canal boats, from Henrik Ibsen's home town of Skien on the coast along the 100-year-old Telemark canal to Dalen in Bandak.

*Dinner is served.*

*Cardemom Town – modelled on a favourite children's story. Kristiansand Zoo.*

*Lyngør. Lille Svalsund.*

Gaustadtoppen, 1883 m. above sea level.

M/S Victoria on its way from Skien to Dalen.

Norwegian peasants invested their savings in silver jewellery to be worn with their national costumes. There was plenty of silver, particularly in Setesdal and Telemark. The oldest silver ornaments were cast or stamped. Filigree came later and was often used for jacket buckles and collar buttons. While silver jewellery varied from place to place, rose-patterned silver ornaments were used all over the country.

*National costume from Vestfold.*

*Above left: National costumes from Meldal and Rennebu.*
*Next page: National costume from Flå.*

# The fjords

*The Nærøy Fjord.*

# THE WEST COUNTRY – REALM OF THE NORWEGIAN FJORDS

*It is the fjords that give the west Norwegian landscape its unique character. The contrasts are enormous. Here mountains drop steeply from snow-covered peaks to the blue waters of the fjord. Nature is both overwhelming and idyllic; solid rivers of ice from the glaciers frame blossoming fruit trees. When you drive along the narrow, winding roads and see how people have scratched a living from the steep mountainsides, you are filled with respect and admiration.*

## Cultural monuments and cultural life

Stave churches are a unique element of the Norwegian architectural heritage from the Middle Ages. Along the Sogn Fjord, the longest fjord in the world, lie five of the best preserved stave churches in the country.

Also from the Middle Ages is Bryggen, the Hanseatic quay in Bergen, a city which otherwise houses a wealth of cultural monuments. Unusual architecture can be seen in Ålesund too, one of the few towns in Europe to be built entirely in the Jugend style. The Bergen International Music Festival is the region's most important annual cultural event, while Molde has also made an international name for itself as host to the annual jazz festival. Apart from these major events, there are a wide range of other cultural activities to choose between.

## Outdoor adventure

Cultural and natural adventures can easily be combined in western Norway. The Geiranger Fjord, Hardanger Fjord and Sogn Fjord are just a ferry trip away from Bergen. And if you are in Molde, you can drive along the exciting

*From Loftus. Girl in national costume from Hardanger*

*Kjeåsen near Eidsfjord.*

## Ferries in the summer night

The realm of the western fjords is linked by a network of ferries, bridges and tunnels. You can travel from the innermost farm in the Sogn Fjord to the outermost fishing village.

*Summer skiing.*

Here too, you will experience strong contrasts. Modern shipyards lie side by side with 19th century fishermen's huts.

Atlantic Ocean Road which winds over islands and rocks across the open sea.

You don't have to be content to just look at the beautiful scenery, you can use it too. Some people climb in it, others walk in it. Those who like fishing can fish in the ocean or cast for salmon in one of the many rivers. In Stryn you can ski in mid-summer, or you can try various other ways of getting around – biking, horseback riding or perhaps rafting down the rapids.

*Guided tours on the glaciers.*

*Drying hay by Lake Lovatn.*

*A barn can be used for so many things before the hay is brought in.*

The Barony in Rosendal.

*Right: Spring in Hardanger. A pink and white symphony of apple blossom against a background of snow-clad mountains and fjords.*

*A Norwegian pony.*

*On the way to the Briksdal Glacier, an arm of the Jostedal Glacier, the biggest glacier on the European continent – by horse and cart.*

*Right: Lake Lovatn.*

*Left: From "The Pulpit" you can look straight down to the*
*Lyse Fjord, 600 metres below.*
*The sky feels close in this kind of situation.*
*Right: Kjeraggen in Lysebotn.*

# BERGEN
# – CAPITAL
# OF THE WESTERN FJORDS

*A port and trading centre ringed by seven mountains,*
*Bergen is a town of flowering rhododendrons and*
*international music festivals. It is also a cultural gem,*
*with wooden architecture, old Hanseatic trading houses*
*on the quay and Troldhaugen, the home of Edvard Grieg.*
*Bergen is the indisputable capital of the beautiful western fjords.*

## An international monument

The unique architecture on the Bergen waterfront has given Bergen a place on UNESCO's World Heritage List. Today "Bryggen" comprises shops, handicraft workshops, artists' studios, restaurants and the Hanseatic Museum.

Three hundred years after the Viking king, Olav Kyrre, had made Bergen capital of Norway, a German Hanseatic trading office in the 14th century brought Bergen back to life as a trading centre. The town has therefore traditionally been an international crossroads.

## Tradition and culture

Perhaps that is why Bergen has so many art collections and museums. It also has one of the oldest symphony orchestras in the world and can pride itself on having fostered playwright Ludvig Holberg, landscape painter J. C. Dahl and virtuoso violinist Ole Bull.

And of course Edvard Grieg, an obvious historical focus for the annual Bergen International Music Festival which takes place in many venues, including the Grieg Hall and the composer's home, Troldhaugen.

*From Bryggen*
*– the old quay in Bergen.*

*A seal in the Bergen aquarium*

*The cable car to Ulriken.*

## Town, fjord and mountains

In 1990, Bergen was voted the cleanest town in Norway and came third in the competition for the "Tidiest City in Europe". A walk in Bergen is a historical tour of old streets and cobbled alleys, small bakeries and cafés. Along the quayside, local ferries and cruise ships lie alongside the sailing ship "Statsraad Lehmkuhl". The charming fish market is in the centre of town, and a ride up the mountain by cable car or to the top of Bergen's highest peak, Ulriken, provides wonderful views of the town, the fjord and the mountains.

*A summer day at Zacharias Quay.*

His fa
comp
comp
Cope
refus
work
that i
Neve
has b
recor
strict
than

**Lon
esse**

T h
E
talen
poor
coun
indep
long
Norw
with
of un
the sa

*"Dancing in Setesdal". Painting by Gustav Wenzel, 1891.*
*Below: A Hardanger fiddle.*

international piano repertoire and has in many ways become a symbol of Norwegianness.

## Abroad to find inspiration

Like so many other contemporary Norwegian painters and poets, Grieg had to leave his homeland and go to Europe to find inspiration. Edvard Munch and Henrik Ibsen went to Germany, France and Italy and benefited artistically from their travels.

*The Grieg Hall.*

Edvard Grieg's first biographer, Aimar Grønvold, concluded that there is a warm, insoluble relationship between the environment in which Grieg lived and the music he wrote.

### Success and defeat

However, success did not come easily. Neither the general public nor professional musicians showed particular interest in the unusual, dissonant harmonies of his composi- tions. They were having a hard enough time understanding the music of Mozart and Beethoven. For many years, Grieg therefore had to be content with com- posing during his summer holidays. For the rest of the year, he was busy earning a living for his family as a choirmaster, orchestra conductor, teacher and performer in Christiania. In 1868, he presented his first great masterpiece, the A minor piano concerto. Grieg was only 25 years old, but had already gained important experience in the art of instrumentation. The concerto is still part of the

So did Edvard Grieg. He travelled abroad at regular intervals, and in 1869 spent a travel grant on a journey to Italy, where he met Franz Liszt and other musicians in Rome's inspiring artistic community.

Grieg's interest in European cities was also due to his need for a larger musical market than he could find in Norway and Scandinavia. Sales of his "Lyric Pieces" made Edvard Grieg's name and music known in Europe and he was soon nicknamed "The Chopin of the North".

## The composer's home, "Troldhaugen"

In 1874, Grieg was awarded a state grant which provided a steady income and moved back to his home town of Bergen. In 1885, he purchased a beautiful house in the Swiss style called "Troldhaugen", overlooking Lake Nordås. From then until his death in 1907, Grieg spent every summer at Troldhaugen. Every winter he toured Europe with his wife, Nina. He was much in demand as a pianist and conductor all over the world, and became a musical ambassador for Norway.

*Above: Troldhaugen.*
*Above left: The score of "Åse's Death".*
*Left: Interior from Troldhaugen.*

When Edvard Grieg died, he was buried at Troldhaugen and his home was converted into a living museum. The interior of the house and the cabin where he worked are authentic. The Steinway grand he was given for a silver wedding present in 1892 still stands in the drawing room and is used today for special concerts.

*Trollstigen – the Troll's Ladder – snakes down the mountainside in an endless series of hairpin bends.*

*Next page: The mountain peaks Bispen, Kongen and Dronningen.*

At Herdalssetra, the biggest goat farm in the region, modern dairy farming methods are used in a two-hundred-year-old mountain farm settlement. Herdalssetra lies 500 metres above sea level, close to beautiful Lake Herdal.

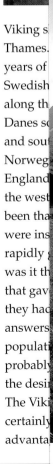

Viking s
Thames.
years of
Swedish
along th
Danes s
and sout
Norweg
England
the west
been tha
were ins
rapidly g
was it th
that gav
they had
answers
populati
probably
the desi
The Viki
certainly
advanta

### Monuments to the Papacy

One of the strange things about the history of the stave churches is that they were "re-discovered" in the 19th century, not by Norwegian churchgoers but by painters of the Romantic period. Their search for memorials of heathen and heroic times – such as burial mounds, ships and runes – led them to the fjords and small villages of the west country. The stave churches had stood there for hundreds of years, irritating local Lutheran congregations by reminding them that it was the Roman Catholic Church that had brought Christianity to Norway. Painters such as Johs. Flintoe and I. C. Dahl were overjoyed to find these hidden treasures and played their part in arousing national and international interest in stave churches.

### Forerunners of the cathedrals?

The Danish-born painter Flintoe drew sketches of the stave churches at Urnes, Borgund and Heddal and wrote the following:
"... of Saxon or Germanic origin, perhaps mother of the later so perfect Gothic style ...". He therefore anticipated the subsequent discussion of the stave church as a possible forerunner

*Borgund Stave Church.*

*Carving at Urnes Stave Church.*

# STAVE CHURCHES

*Norwegian stave churches may be regarded as architectural monuments to the meeting of Christianity with Norse paganism. In these modest but nevertheless, for their time, monumental buildings, the Roman Catholic faith merged with the animal ornamentation of the Viking Age and Norwegian wood-carving traditions.*

of the great cathedrals of northern Europe.

This was the beginning of the registration of remaining stave churches which began in the 19th century. First came the architects, then the Society for the Preservation of Norwegian Ancient Monuments and finally the art and architecture historians. They faced a formidable task. Approximately twenty stave churches had survived the devastation of time, the lack of historical understanding and deficient maintenance.

In the course of 200 years, 1200 such churches were built in

# THE VIKINGS

*"Deliver us, oh God, from the rage of the Vikings," people prayed in the monasteries and churches of Normandy in the ninth century. The Vikings came from the sea like a flock of wolves. They burned and raped, pillaged and murdered, from the Caspian Sea in the east to Ireland in the west. With their graceful, seaworthy ships, they crossed the Atlantic to Greenland in the north and sailed along the Mediterranean to Constantinople (Istanbul) in the south.*

The Oseberg ship, AD 834.

Head of a monster from the Oseberg find, AD 834.

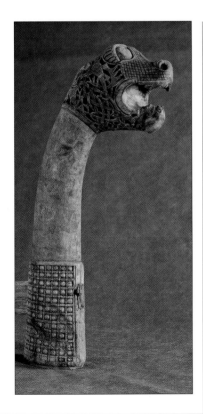

## Warriors and explorers

The Vikings dressed in skins and rough cloth, wore iron helmets on their heads and were covered in fleas and lice. They must have looked terrifying. But they were also capable seamen who sailed in uncharted waters. The Vikings discovered America five hundred years before Columbus and set foot on the small volcanic island of Iceland long before anyone else, with the possible exception of a handful of Irish monks. The Vikings also colonised the Irish capital, Dublin, and the city of York in northern England. Nevertheless, they are primarily remembered in Europe as warriors and plunderers. Archaeological finds show that there had been contacts between the Nordic peoples and the rest of Europe since ancient times. So what was it that changed peaceful traders into raiders at the end of the eighth century and suddenly caused the Scandinavian Vikings to attack the countries in the south so aggressively?

## Ocean-going landing craft

The Viking raids began with three ships. In 836 there were 25 ships and in winter 850 it is said that there were 350

medieval Norway. In other words, the country was converted to Christianity in a very short period of time, and an average of six churches were consecrated each year for 200 years.

## Many small churches

The Norwegian King Olav Haraldsson is often credited with the honour of having brought Christianity to Norway. Whatever the case, it is certain that after his death at the Battle of Stiklestad in 1030, Christianity rapidly found a foothold all over the country. Numerous churches were built by local communities. The churches therefore reflect local building traditions, and they were constructed from the materials that were to hand, in other words wood rather than stone.

In his work "Stavkirker" (Stave Churches, Grøndahl & Dreyer, 1994), Gunnar Bugge writes that there is nothing we can call a "Norwegian" Roman or Gothic architectural style. The independent Norwegian character appears to be a continuation, a refinement of foundations laid in the Viking Age, transferred to the area of church architecture. The discoveries of the Vikings and the Norwegian seafarers on the European continent were brought back as impulses to be matured and methods and materials to be re-used and developed.

*Heddal Stave Church.*

*Above: Urnes Stave Church.*

*Left: Hopperstad Stave Church.*

## New building techniques

The first churches to be built in Norway in the 11th century, the so-called Missionary Age, literally had unsound foundations. The staves were placed directly in holes in the ground, and in less than a hundred years, the corner posts had rotted and the church was ruined. Archaeological excavations have uncovered holes containing the rotten remains of wooden poles which show where the first churches stood. In the new churches, the staves and planks stood on horizontal beams.

In this way, the church wall was raised from the ground and protected against damp and rot. Vertical wooden poles – staves – are mainly found in western Norway, while in south-eastern Norway horizontal cogged logs intersect to provide protection against the colder climate.

## Dragons' heads and wood carving

Many of the Norwegian stave churches are richly decorated. The portals in particular are unique works of art for which the best contemporary wood carving techniques were used. Dragons and dragons' heads are recurrent motifs, as are vines and leaves. However, there is little to indicate that this type of

decoration had any Christian message or significance. Gunnar Bugge writes in his book "Stavkirker" that, apart from being used for halls for kings or chiefs, the stave method was probably also used for the construction of *hov* – small heathen temples for private or public use. The *hov* were often re-consecrated as Christian churches. Otherwise the congregation had to tear down the *hov* and build a new church. Perhaps this is one of the reasons why the stave churches are dark and gloomy and have an almost mystical atmosphere, small round windows high under the roof being the only sources of light. Here visitors can sense a breath of the Norwegian Middle Ages, of the Roman Catholic faith and of Norwegian Viking traditions.

*Left and below: Borgund Stave Church.*
*Below left: Nore Stave Church.*

# The mountains

*Hunderfossen.*

# TROLL PARK
# – MOUNTAINS AND
# CULTURAL TREASURES

*Troll Park is the new name for the heart of Norway, the mountainous inland region in the south-east. From the Olympic towns of Lillehammer, Hamar and Gjøvik, everything is within reach: beautiful Valdres, cultural treasures at the Maihaugen outdoor museum, Dovrefjell national park, Bjørnstjerne Bjørnson's home at Aulestad and Norway's highest mountain, Galdhøpiggen, in the centre of Jotunheimen – Home of the Giants. This is the background for such well-known characters in world literature as Kristin Lavransdatter and Peer Gynt.*

## Excitement and relaxation in natural surroundings

The Norwegians live an active outdoor life and here in the heart of the country there are opportunities for many different activities, both for those seeking excitement and challenge and those who prefer

*Maihaugen.*

*Lillehammer.*

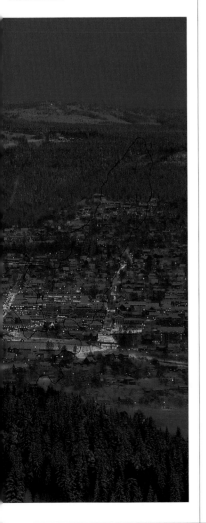

## Rural culture and antiques, Olympic venues and sporting activities

There's plenty of ancient architecture and rural art in this part of Norway. At Maihaugen, an outdoor museum at Lillehammer which houses a collection of 150 ancient buildings, you can learn more about this part of the Norwegian cultural heritage.

Lillehammer lies at the northern end of Lake Mjøsa, the biggest lake in Norway. In summer, Skibladner, the oldest paddle steamer in the world, will take you to all three Olympic towns. In Hamar you can see one of the most exciting examples of modern Norwegian wooden architecture, the ice rink where the speed skating championships took place during the 1994 Winter Olympics, popularly known as the Viking Ship. If you cross Lake Mjøsa to

*Skibladner on Lake Mjøsa, the biggest lake in Norway.*

peace and tranquillity.

You can go mountain climbing in Jotunheimen or rafting in ideal conditions on fast-flowing rivers. Or you can walk along marked trails through peaceful forests and across open mountain plateaux. The lakes of Femundmarka offer rich fishing. On the mountain glaciers you can go skiing in midsummer. And in autumn you can experience the magnificent colours in the Dovre mountains on a clear day, or wander among blueberries and mushrooms in the Trysil forests and watch nature settling down for the long winter ahead.

*Rafting on the Sjoa.*

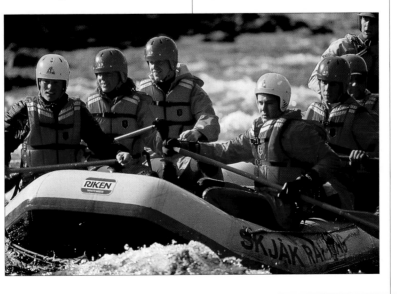

Gjøvik, you will find another interesting Olympic arena, the Olympic Cavern Hall. As its name indicates, it was blasted out of the mountain using engineering skills that have aroused international interest. Here it is possible to go skating or try the climbing wall. The Olympic arenas were built with future use in mind. In winter, the alpine venues and the cross country trails in the Olympic region are open to everyone. Lillehammer is also the home of the Hunderfossen family park, which offers a children's adventure swimming pool, model car tracks, Norway's only waxwork museum and Ivo Caprino's fairy tale grotto with its unique collection of Caprino puppets, used in the filming Norwegian fairy tales.

Tourist brochures abound with clichés about Norwegian nature. "Europe's last wilderness", "untouched, original and genuine". And let's face it, there are reasons for using words like this. You can go more or less anywhere you like. There are few fences and plenty of footpaths.

For many Norwegians, hunting and outdoor life are inextricably linked. Every autumn, thousands of hunters go to the mountains. For most of them it doesn't matter whether they catch much. It's the social contact with fellow hunters, the fresh mountain air and the feeling of freedom that count.

*Reindeer.*

*Grouse in summer plumage.*

*Black bearberries.*

*Above: Moose*

*Right: Bear*

*Below: Bluethroat*

# EAST OF THE SUN AND WEST OF THE MOON

## – Norwegian trolls and fairy tales

*Who has not seen the silhouette of a ragged troll in an outcrop of rock?
Or the staring eye of Nøkken, the river sprite, among the water-lilies
in a dark forest pool? And of course the Norwegian domestic goblin
lives in the barn. Every child in Norway knows that.*

*The Norwegian domestic goblin.*

The beautiful, rugged Norwegian landscape conceals sprites and elves, goblins and trolls, talking foxes and a beautiful female troll called Huldra. The only thing that distinguishes her from human beings is her long tail. This is the land of Norwegian fairy tales; the land east of the sun and west of the moon.

## Folk stories from the depths of time

For many generations, the minds of Norwegian children have been filled with pictures of goblins and huldras, of Askeladden who beat a troll in an eating competition and won the princess and half the kingdom, of the mill that stands at the bottom of the sea and grinds salt, and of the three billy goats gruff who were to walk to the mountains to get fat and had to conquer the ugly troll who lived under the bridge. All these fairytale characters come from the treasure chest of Norwegian folk stories. The fairy tales and legends have travelled from mouth to mouth, from family to family, from generation to generation.

Not until the 19th century were systematic efforts made to collect all this oral material. The pioneers in Norway were P. Chr. Asbjørnsen and Jørgen Moe. Their ideals were the German brothers, Jacob and Wilhelm Grimm.
The German fairy tale collectors made great efforts to be true to the folk tradition, and Asbjørnsen and Moe followed their example.

## International stories

Asbjørnsen and Moe published several collections of fairy tales which have subsequently become classic examples of the Norwegian fairy tale tradition. Their names are as famous as the Grimm brothers in Germany or Hans Christian Andersen in Denmark. Asbjørnsen and Moe demonstrated a deep under-

*P. Chr. Asbjørnsen*

*Jørgen Moe*

standing of the value of fairy tales. They were not satisfied with collecting them; they retold them – "faithfully as we have received them from the narrator.....". The stories emerged in a new linguistic guise which is still regarded as exemplary today. But were the fairy tales they gathered Norwegian?

There is little to suggest that their roots are exclusively Norwegian. Fairy tales and folk legends are among the most international of all literary genres. In Norway, however, they were given their own expression and quality, and characteristically Norwegian personalities. Typical of the

Norwegian fairy tales is their realistic, objective narrative style which contains no emotions or ornamental details.

## The wizard who drew trolls

The content of the text was deepened, enlarged and brought to life by the illustrations. No artist has illustrated Norwegian fairy tales with more imaginative understanding than Theodor Kittelsen. Hardly anyone in Norway today fails to recognise his drawings or his style.

*Theodor Kittelsen:*
*"Soria Moria Castle", 1900.*
*"I have little, but we shall share since you are so needy," said Askeladden.*

*Theodor Kittelsen:*
*"Nøkken", 1904.*

*Theodor Kittelsen:*

*"Peer Gynt in the hall of the mountain king", 1913.*

*Theodor Kittelsen:*

*"The hare laughed so much that his jaw cracked", 1884.*

*Theodor Kittelsen*

the stories came from. "And the forest gave us the fairy tale," he writes in his book "Troldskap" (Magic) which was published in Christiania in 1916.

That is why all Norwegians know what a huldra looks like, and *Nøkken* the river sprite, the trolls, the subterranean goblins, the fairy Soria Moria palace and the princess on the back of the polar bear White Bear King Valemon. Kittelsen's artistic use of his medium, with black and white extremes and a range of greys in between, is in a class on its own in the history of Norwegian drawing.

The painter Christian Krogh wrote of Kittelsen "One is imprisoned and spirited into an

With artistic prowess, he added eyes, arms and legs to roots, stumps and mountains, made them move – and created trolls. Kittelsen was himself a man of the forests and mountains, and he was in no doubt about where

*Theodor Kittelsen:*

*"The troll who wonders how old he is",* *1911.*

*Theodor Kittelsen:*
*"Kvitebjørn Kong Valemon", 1912.*

church bells and burst or turn into stone if they are exposed to sunlight. They are vanquished by the poor, inventive, good-hearted Askeladden, who finally wins the captive princess and half the kingdom.

But Norwegian fairy tales are about more than trolls. The main characters are often wild or domestic animals who talk and behave like human beings. The bear, the fox and the wolf feature frequently, as do domestic animals like cats, goats and hens. The best known fairy tale in Norway is about the three billy goats gruff who are going to the mountains to get fat in the summer pastures. Nevertheless, most of the stories are about witches, giants and trolls. Or about human beings with superhuman powers. The magic fairy tales tell of the boy with the seven league boots, tablecloths which constantly fill with food, golden castles and other fantastic objects. And about people who can turn into animals or other creatures. One of the best known fairy tales, "East of the sun and west of the moon", has roots going right back to the Greek myth of Amor and Psyche.

entirely new world where one feels, suffers, sees with him, this intense man who walks alone with open eyes and receptive nerves in the large, pure, natural wilderness."

## Witches and trolls

Trolls have a special place in Norwegian fairy tales. They live in the forests and mountains, are enormously large, ugly and stupid, but can smell Christian blood from a long distance. They like princesses and keep them prisoner in the mountains if they have the chance. Trolls cannot tolerate the sound of

# Central Norway

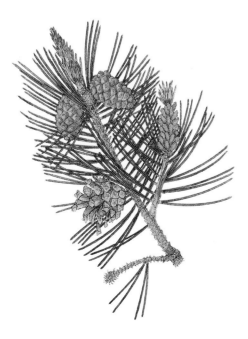

with other historical treasures. Trøndelag has a rich variety of other monuments too, including medieval churches, ruined monasteries and the renaissance castle Austrått. In spite of all its historical roots, Trondheim is today a modern city with an interesting waterfront, museums, and cultural festivals in ancient and modern surroundings.

# OUTDOOR PARADISE IN CENTRAL NORWAY

*The Trøndelag counties are a natural paradise. Here the Atlantic Ocean breaks on the coast and the islands. Fjords cut deep into the landscape, and behind them lie farms, large forests and mountain plateaux. People hunt and fish more here than any other place in Norway. Trøndelag has played an important historical role, and the Nidaros Cathedral, the largest cathedral in the Nordic countries, is an impressive monument. In 1997, Trondheim will be celebrating its millennium as a town and capital of central Norway.*

## On historic ground

Trøndelag played a particularly important role in Norwegian history during the Middle Ages. One of the most important events was the Battle of Stiklestad in 1030 where King Olav was killed. Olav was later regarded as a saint and the Nidaros Cathedral was raised due to St. Olav's importance to pilgrims from all over Europe. The crown jewels are also kept in Nidaros Cathedral, together

## Mountains, fjords and ocean

From the musk oxen in the Dovrefjell national park to the wild bears in the mountain municipality of Lierne, from the deer on the island of Hitra to the salmon fisherman's paradise Namsskogan, Trøndelag is a fascinating place for anyone who is seeking untouched natural wilderness. Ski enthusiasts can enjoy alpine skiing at Oppdal and salt water fishermen can travel to Vikna and catch large cod in the ocean.

*Nidaros Cathedral, Trondheim.*

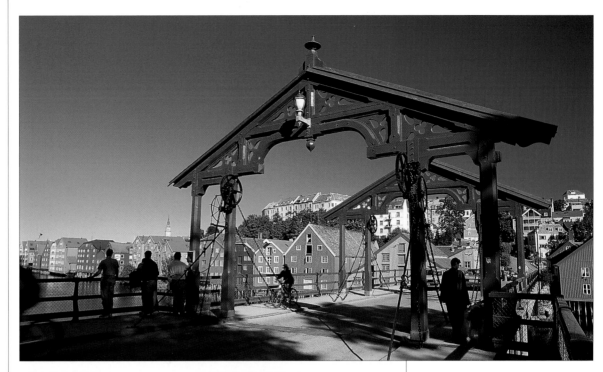

*The old town bridge in Trondheim.*

## The mining town of Røros

The Røros copper mines were once one of the largest industrial enterprises in Northern Europe. The last copper mine closed in 1986 after 342 years of mining operations. The 300-year-old wooden houses and the old mining town are a unique cultural monument and are included on UNESCO's World Heritage List.

The mountain town of Røros is a living museum, and the Olav mine from 1650 is still open to visitors.

# NORWAY – THE CRADLE OF SKIING

*Girl from Setesdal, 1889.*

*"Skiing is the most national of all Norwegian sports, and a wonderful sport it is – if anything deserves to be called the sport of sports, this must be it,"* wrote Fridtjof Nansen after he had crossed the Greenland icecap on skis from east to west in 1888.

*The Winter Olympics, Lillehammer 1994.*
*Closing ceremony.*

## Viking kings on skis

In the Viking Age, skis were a normal means of transport and many kings have been described as good skiers, including King Harald, Olav Trygvason and St. Olav. But none of them have been able to measure up to the Sami people. In ancient accounts by Icelander Snorre Sturluson and Saxo Grammaticus, the Sami are described as being the best skiers in the Nordic countries. "The Lapps were so good at skiing that neither men nor animals could compete with them for speed," Laurentius Urdahl quotes the old historians in his "Haandbog i Skiløbning" (Skiing Handbook) from 1893. The heroic lays of Nordic mythology also tell of skiing and hunting and often feature Ull, the god of skiing and Skade, the goddess of hunting.

## Father of modern ski sports

There are many historical accounts of how priests, postmen and the kings' soldiers – in the form of ski companies – used skis in the 18th century. But skiing did not become a popular sport until the end of the 19th century. The man behind this new interest in skiing, Sondre Norheim, was born in the village of Morgedal, Telemark, in 1825.

Norheim revolutionised skiing when he started using stiff willow bindings round his heels. He also constructed a ski with curved sides, the Telemark ski. With his new technique, he could turn and jump without the skis falling off, and he was regarded as an excellent skier by his contemporaries.

Sondre Norheim conquered the Norwegian capital, Christiania during the first national skiing championships in 1867 with his ski jumping and slalom prowess.

The word "slalom" also comes from Morgedal. The first syllable, "sla" means slope, hill or smooth surface, while "låm" is a downhill track. An ordinary slalom was a cross country trail

*Sondre Norheim*

which crossed fields and stone walls and ran between trees and bushes.

Telemark skiing is in fashion again and has re-emerged as a popular leisure activity in Europe and the USA.

## Out into the world with skis on their feet

Skiing as a sport became highly popular as a result of Norwegians practising their old sport in new countries. Norwegian architecture and engineering students in Germany, Switzerland, France and Austria made skiing popular. The first skiing competition in Germany, at Tauenberg near Munich in 1895, was organised on the initiative of Norwegian students. Fridtjof Nansen's book *På ski over Grønland* (The First Crossing of Greenland) was published in most European languages in 1890 and further increased interest in skiing. However, Norwegian emigrants had brought skiing to the USA as early as 1825. Jon Torsteinson Rui from Telemark (Snowshoe Thompson) was an innovator who used skis to keep the mail route open across the Sierra Nevada.

## Popular sport for exercise and competition

Norwegians often boast that they are born with skis on their feet. Norway's four million plus population actually has 30,000 kilometres of marked ski trails at its disposal in the forests and mountains. That's three times the distance from Norway to Australia. There are 2,500 floodlit ski trails all over the country where people can relax after work on dark winter evenings. And, as if this were not enough, when winter is receding and the spring sunshine warms the country, half the population goes to the mountains at Easter to enjoy the last of the snow before summer arrives

So perhaps it's not surprising that Norwegians make their mark on polar expeditions and do well at cross country, alpine skiing, ski jumping and biathlon events. The Winter Olympics at Lillehammer gave foreign tourists and millions of TV viewers all over the world a glimpse of Norway's winter wonderland.

# Northern Norway

# Northern Norway – Arctic nights and midday sun

*When the winter night lasts all day and the sun never sets in summer, life has a different quality. That's how it is in northern Norway, at least when winter is at its darkest and summer at its lightest. People and nature are different up here. There is nothing small about the ocean, the plains or the people; Northern Norway is a spacious, generous place.*

## Rugged, beautiful scenery

North Norway is one of the most untouched places in Europe. So far north, conditions are more extreme than further south and people have had to adapt. Today, visitors can live in a Sami tent on the Finnmark plains or a fisherman's hut in the Lofoten islands and experience what this means. A whale safari or a trip on the plains in a reindeer sled also leave a lasting impression. From North Cape, the northernmost point in Europe, you can look out across the Barents Sea towards Svalbard and the North Pole.

*Lofoten.*

*Svartisen (the Black Ice) is the second largest glacier in Norway.*

## Hamsunesque landscape

The North Norwegian landscape has influenced the works of Nobel Prizewinner Knut Hamsun. His birthplace, Hamarøy, and the old trading post at Kjerringøy are familiar from several of his novels. This is where Hamsun's characters wandered restlessly in the summer night.

The town of Svolvær in Lofoten has attracted many famous painters who have been fascinated by the unique light and colours. But they have not only painted landscapes. The hard-working fishermen have also been portrayed on canvas. For if nature can be beautiful, the struggle for survival has often been harsh and brutal. The men who provided the raw material for the dried fish which has been northern Norway's main source of income for centuries lived a dangerous life.

### The Paris of the North and Sami art

On the way to Bodø on the ferry along the coastal highway, you can see the Svartisen glacier, which creeps right down to the sea, and killer whales playing around the ship's sides.

In Tromsø, known as the Paris of the North because of its cafés, restaurants and lively night life, lies the majestic Arctic Cathedral. In Bodø, Tromsø and Harstad there are jazz, film and cultural festivals all the year round.

Kautokeino lies on the Finnmark plateau and is the largest Sami community in the world. The area populated by the Sami people stretches all across the Arctic region, across the northern areas of Norway, Sweden, Finland and into Russia. In Kautokeino you can experience the unique life, handicrafts and silversmiths' art of the Sami people at close quarters.

*Right: Svolvær.*

Norway has always been a major fish exporter for two reasons. Firstly, there is plenty of fish, and secondly, fish is conserved simply and effectively. It is dried in the open air, and once it is dry it can be kept for several years. There has always been plenty of demand for this first-class product.

*Puffin.*

Today two cultures live side by side in northern Norway, the Sami and the Norwegian. Both the languages and the lifestyles are very different. Of course, most people have now been absorbed by the melting pot we call the European cultural heritage, but there are still families who live in the traditional way, with reindeer farming as their only source of income.

*Left: Northern lights over the Finnmark plateau.*

### Svalbard

Svalbard has three national parks, two nature reserves, three plant conservation areas and fifteen bird sanctuaries. Tourists visiting Svalbard can experience this wonderland by dog sled, snow scooter, on skis or from a canoe. The archipelago has an exciting wildlife but only four species of land mammal: the polar bear, the polar fox, the Svalbard reindeer and the fieldmouse. Male polar bears may be hungry and curious, so travelling in the wilderness can be dangerous. Svalbard has 163 registered bird species although only 25–30 of them nest regularly. The ocean around the islands is a playground for many Arctic marine mammals, including several whale species which have survived former

# SVALBARD – NORTHERN WILDERNESS

*Svalbard is an Arctic archipelago located at 81 degrees north, close to the Arctic Circle. The islands are a mixture of national parks and nature reserves, modern mining operations, traditional hunting and fishing communities, tourist attractions and an Arctic research station.*

exploitation. Today there are about 1,000 walrus after the walrus became a protected species in 1952.

### Whaling, down and eggs

Icelandic sources indicate that Svalbard – the country with the cold coasts – may have been discovered by Norwegians in 1194. This Arctic archipelago was certainly included on the Arctic maps after Dutchman Willem Barents went ashore there in 1596. Due to the high, pointed mountains, he called the country Spitzbergen. This discovery paved the way for large-scale whaling expeditions, with the Dutch and British leading the way, although Norwegians, French, Basques and whalers from the Hanseatic towns also took part. Russian hunters travelled to Svalbard from the beginning of the 18th century to collect eggs and down, and to hunt reindeer and walrus for their fur. Norwegian seal hunters also experienced many good years on Svalbard, which reached their peak at the end of the last century. At the beginning of this century, coal was discovered on the islands, which triggered renewed competition for Svalbard's natural resources.

## Svalbard's black gold

Mining led to the industrialisation of the Arctic islands and until World War I the Americans, British, Dutch, Russians and Norwegians all exploited the coal reserves. The competition for black gold soon led to conflicts about mining rights and sovereignty.

After negotiations, the Svalbard Treaty was ratified by the nations concerned in 1920. Under this treaty, Norway was given sovereignty over the archipelago and on 14 August 1925, Svalbard became part of the Kingdom of Norway. More than 40 countries have signed and ratified the treaty, which gives the citizens of signatory powers equal rights to pursue economic activities and forbids defence installations and naval bases on the islands.

Today, only Norway and Russia are involved in coal mining operations. The two countries produce a total of approximately one million tons of coal a year. Widespread oil and gas exploration has been carried out on Svalbard but no viable discoveries have been made. On the other hand, the drilling has provided valuable information about the geology of the islands.

## The history of the Earth's development in one place

The coast of Spitzbergen, with its jagged mountains, fjords and glaciers, can take any visitor's breath away. Monacofjellet (1,084 m above sea level) and Tyskertoppen (1,012 m above sea level) are the highest peaks on the west coast. This beautiful, rugged scenery is both tempting and frightening. Svalbard's landscape changes according to the geological structure, and the sediment layers contain fossils which enable us to follow the history of the Earth's development more continuously than in most other parts of the world. Almost sixty per cent of Svalbard's 63,000 square metres is covered by permanent ice. Many of the glaciers stretch right down to the coast, where they "calve", leaving large icebergs in the sea.

On land, the permafrost in coastal areas reaches down to 100 metres and inland it is 500 metres deep.

## Tourism and environmental conservation

Just under 4,000 people live on Svalbard. Of these, 2,500 are foreigners, mainly Russians. Longyearbyen, which is the administrative centre of the archipelago, has a population of about 1,000. The Norwegian Governor acts as county governor, chief of police and notary public. Due to its location, Svalbard has a unique position. The islands and the seas around them are the most accessible of all the Arctic regions. Thanks to the warm currents of the Gulf Stream, Svalbard has a milder climate than its location might indicate. Every year, approximately 25 cruise ships visit Svalbard carrying a total of 15–20,000 tourists. SAS and Braathens SAFE airlines run daily flights between Tromsø and Longyearbyen and rather less frequent local flights to Ny Ålesund, where the Norwegian Polar Institute has one of the most northerly permanent research stations in the world.

Mining activities, arctic research and adventure tourism are all subject to strict regulation in order to protect the vulnerable natural environment and conserve cultural monuments, such as the many centuries old Norwegian and Russian hunting and research stations.

*Polar bears.*

### Hunters, farmers and city dwellers

When Norwegians are asked what are the most typical Norwegian delicacies, most people answer meat balls, mutton and cabbage stew, and cod. However, modern Norwegian cuisine is a mixture of a hunter's menu of fish and game, traditional farm fare, and continental food traditions introduced by the bourgeoisie in the 18th century. Nevertheless, as elsewhere in Europe, there are major regional differences in specialities and the use of raw materials – from the coast inland and from the north to the south of Norway.

While southern Europeans in the Middle Ages were steaming shells and crustaceans in white wine, the Norwegians were throwing them back into the sea or using them as bait. We ate porridge, dried fish and smoked meat. And drank beer, of course. The salt that was used to preserve food had to be imported from other countries, usually by traders. In the Viking Age it was also much-prized booty, as the poor inhabitants of Noirmoutier in France discovered.

### From herring and potatoes to Chinese takeaways

While the transition to arable farming and animal husbandry changed food

# NORWEGIAN FOOD – FROM NATURE'S OWN LARDER

*Norwegians didn't begin to use forks on a daily basis until 1850, several centuries after the rest of Europe. We still swear by our packed lunches – slices of bread and cheese or meat – which we eat for lunch and on ski trips. And at Christmas we insist on eating lutefisk, which is dried cod soaked in caustic soda and served with bacon fat and stewed peas. But Norwegian cuisine is more than packed lunches and lutefisk.*

traditions to a certain extent, the major revolution came with the advent of the potato in the 18th century. It saved many from starvation in fishing and farming communities that were exposed to a cold climate and variable supplies of resources. For many centuries, meat, fish, bread, milk, butter and cheese were the staple foods of the average Norwegian diet, with the addition of potatoes and herring. The latter was called the silver of the sea and was poor man's fare for many centuries. Today, herring is as expensive as any other fish and is mostly cured or pickled. Continental food traditions did not gain ground in the cities until the 19th and 20th

centuries, when they influenced the use of spices, wine and new raw materials. Today, various immigrant cultures have also made their mark on Norwegian eating habits. There are Chinese, Indian and Mexican restaurants all over the country, to mention just a few examples of ethnic cuisine.

### Raw materials from nature's own larder

Norwegian cuisine today is based on both imported and domestically produced ingredients. The latter are often more expensive than imported goods, for due to climatic conditions it is impossible to compete in price with products from countries further south. On the other hand, Norwegian raw materials are of very high quality and Norwegian fruit, berries and vegetables have an excellent flavour.

In addition to high quality ingredients, Norwegian cuisine can offer cured specialities, for instance *fenalår* (cured leg of mutton) and cured ham, cured fish, smoked salmon, and Lofoten cod garnished with roe and liver. And nature provides game too: grouse, venison, moose and much else besides. Apart from all this, there is the special cuisine associated with the culture of the Sami reindeer farmers in northern and southern Norway. Reindeer meat plays a central role, in the form of boiled, roast and smoked meats and entrails. The best known Sami specialities include smoked reindeer meat with marrow bone, tongue and bouillon, and *finnbiff*, which consists of fine slivers of reindeer meat fried in butter with sour cream and goat's cheese.

## Cheese, salmon, aquavit and Bocuse d'Or

Norway is best known abroad for a handful of exported products. They include Jarlsberg cheese, aquavit, a strong liquor made from potatoes and caraway seeds, and fresh farmed salmon. If we had had the opportunity, we would probably have exported milk too, for Norwegians are in no doubt that they produce the best milk in the world. Every Norwegian drinks 150 litres of milk a year.

With the growing internationalisation of Norwegian cuisine, Norwegian chefs have also become increasingly recognised abroad. Chef Bent Stiansen won the Bocuse d'Or in 1993 and Arne Brimi, the master chef from Lom, has specialised in combining continental cuisine with national and regional specialities.

Although today you can drink imported beer from Germany, Jamaica, Spain, Mexico and the

USA, beer has a thousand-year history in Norway. The Vikings drank their home-brewed *mungåt*, the strong *bjorr* and the festive *mjød*, which was made from hops, water, honey and sweetened spices.

Spirits came to Norway in the 16th century and were long regarded as medicine because they were mixed with herbs. Aquavit is the Christmas beverage for most Norwegians, and beer is usually used as a chaser. This is a mixture which foreigners are well advised not to try.

We are not descended from the Vikings for nothing!

© N.W. Damm & Søn AS
N-0055 OSLO
www.touristbooks.com
E-mail: trude.solheim@damm.no
Tel: +47 24 05 10 00
Fax: +47 24 05 12 92
Cover design: Skomsøy Grønli AS
Page design: Junn Paasche-Aasen
Art Director: Bård Løken
Translations: Berlitz GlobalNET
Printed by Narayana Press,
Denmark 2003
8. printing 2003

Texts to full page illustrations:

*Flyleaf page 1: Hardanger fiddle*

*Flyleaf page 2: Score of Edvard Grieg's A minor concerto.*

*Flyleaf page 3: Heather in bloom.*

*Page 2–3: The Geiranger Fjord with Skageflå farm and the Seven Sisters waterfalls.*

*Page 4–5: Autumn morning in the mountains. Døråldalen in Rondane.*

*Page 6–7: The old town, Stavanger.*

*Page 8–9: Henningsvær in the fishing season, Lofoten.*

*Page 10: Hardanger bride.*

*Page 25: Strømstangen lighthouse, outer Oslo Fjord.*

*Page 30–31: Winter evening at Lutvann, Oslo.*

*Page 40: Lindesnes lighthouse.*

*Page 46: "Blindleia" near Lillesand.*

*Page 54: The Bridal Veil waterfall in the Geiranger Fjord.*

*Page 58–59: At the innermost point of the Geiranger Fjord even the biggest cruise ships look small.*

*Page 62–63: Sheep grazing below the Hildal waterfall near Odda.*

*Page 66–67: The Aurland Fjord.*

*Page 74–75: Winter mood in Bergen.*

*Page 82–83: Ålesund.*

*Page 94: Mountain stream in Leirdalen valley, Jotunheimen.*

*Page 100–101: Winter morning at Dønfossen on the River Otta.*

*Page 110–111: Røros. Røros is on the UNESCO World Heritage List.*

*Page 114–115: From old Røros.*

*Page 118: Rock carvings from Alta, "Reindeer hunting".*

*Page 122–123: Reine in Lofoten.*

*Page 126–127: Puffin.*

*Page 130–131: Midnight sun at North Cape.*

SOURCES:

Organisation by Per Erik Borge.

Royal Norwegian Ministry of Foreign Affairs.

Bunader – bakgrunn, rekonstruksjon, bruk (National costumes – background, reconstruction, use). Published by the National Council for Folk Costume.

Folkedrakter, bunader og samiske drakter i Norge (Folk Costumes, National Costumes and Sami Costumes in Norway). Published by the Royal Norwegian Ministry of Foreign Affairs.

I Edvard Munchs fotspor (In Edvard Munch's footsteps). Published by the Munch Museum, Oslo.

Munch-Museet (The Munch Museum). Published by the Municipality of Oslo Art Collections.

Munch – His Life and Works by Marit Lande. Published by Aventura Forlag.

Stavkirker (Stave Churches) by Gunnar Bugge and Bernandino Mezzanotte. Published by Grøndahl og Dreyers Forlag AS.

Th. Kittelsen: Troll i Norge (Th. Kittelsen: Trolls in Norway) by Eli Ketilsson. Published by J. M. Stenersens Forlag AS.

Hekser og Troll (Witches and Trolls) by Åse Moe and Kjellrun Fosmark. Published by Gyldendal Norsk Forlag.

Møter med Th. Kittelsen (Meetings with Th. Kittelsen), Holger Kofoed (ed.). Published by Gyldendal Norsk Forlag.

The Viking. Published by Crescent Books, New York.

Vikingenes visdomsord (Viking words of wisdom) translated by L. Holm-Olsen. Published by Gudrun Publishing AS. J. W. Cappelens Forlag.

Vikingene var voldelige. Vold kostet. (The Vikings were violent. Violence had a price). Published by the University Museum of National Antiquities in Oslo.

Vårt norske kjøkken (Our Norwegian Cuisine), ed. Kjell E. Innli. Published by Svein Gran, KOM Forlag AS.

PHOTOGRAPHS

Above = A    Above left = B
Above right = C    Below = D
Below left = E    Below right = F

*Samfoto:*

Mikael Andersson: 61E

Hans Hvide Bang: 124E

Trym Ivar Bergsmo: 21A, 124B, 130, 131

Espen Bratlie: 15, 24, 25, 17EF, 27CD, 34A, 35AE, 48B, 97B

Jan Arve Dale: 42D, 44AD, 45, 46, 47, 57D, 68C, 73CD, 81C, 87B, 90D

Bernt Eide: 124C

Per Eide: 2, 3, 6, 7, 8, 9, 16A, 58, 59, 69, 70, 71B, 74, 75, 77, 86B, 87C, 111, 113A, 124F

Jon Fjeldstad: 103F

Fred Friberg: 42C

Steve Halsetrønning: 112D

Kim Hart: 26B, 29.

Johannes Haugan: 13, 98F

Steinar Haugberg: 18A

Pål Hermansen: 40, 48CE, 56A, 61F, 93E, 99, 104F

Jon Østeng Hov: 103E

Åsmund Lindal: 41

Rune Lislerud: 21F, 34, 50A, 52F

Bård Løken: 16D, 15A, 19A, 20A, 32, 33, 49, 54, 55, 58, 59, 61A, 62, 63, 64F, 65, 66, 67, 68B, 84F, 85, 90A, 91, 92AD, 94, 95, 100, 101, 113D, 114, 115, 122, 123

J.B. Olsen / R. Sørensen: 76A, 79A, 118

Jørn Areklett Omre: 1, 4, 5, 13, 25, 28AD, 30, 31, 57B, 102, 104C, 105, 110

Dag Røttereng: 103A.

Øystein Søbye: 104E, 132D, 133A

Helge Sunde: 35A, 97C

Stig Tronvold: 21E

Henrik Øyen: 104B


OTHER PHOTOGRAPHS:

Bunader og Samiske folkedrakter. J.W. Cappelens Forlag: 10, 11, 50, 51, 52, 53

Jon Fjeldstad: 125

Great Shots: 133D

Willy Haraldsen: 13, 43C, 48F, 56, 57CD, 64AE, 72AD, 73B, 76D, 80F, 84A, 86D, 96A, 98E.

Kodak: 116D.

Egil Korsnes: 81D

Kristiansen: 82, 83

Håkon Li: 93AF

Thor Melhus: 19D

Kjell E. Midthun: 106

Torbjørn Moen: 121E

National Gallery, Oslo, photo: J. Lathion: Gustav Wentzel: Dancing in Setesdal, 80D; Theodor Kittelsen: Soria Moria Slott, 1900, 107C; Theodor Kittelsen: Nøkken, 1904, 107F

Norwegian Folk Museum, Oslo: 22, 107B

NTB: 22

University Museum of National Antiquities in Oslo.: 88E

Municipality of Oslo Art Collections, Munch Museum: 23, 37, 38, 39

Terje Rakke: 13, 20D, 42B, 43BE, 44EF, 71C, 97D, 119, 112A, 132A

Jarle Kjetil Rolseth: 117C

Ola Røe: 128, 129

Scanfoto: 22, 34E, 35F, 117CD

Maritime Museum, Bergen: 78D

Norwegian Skiing Association: 116B

Ted Spiegel: 88A

Norwegian Mapping Authority: 12

National Gallery, Stockholm: P.S. Krøyer: Nina og Edvard Grieg 79D

Urpo A. Tarnanen: 13, 15, 26D, 32F, 98B

To-Foto: 13

Visioni: 80E, 116B

O. Væring: 89A, 108–109, 116C

Lisa Westgaard: 60, 134, 135


The flower illustrations were drawn by Dagny Tande Lid and lent by the University of Oslo Botanical Gardens and Museum.


Silver Birch, Betula pendula p. 11

Aspen, Populus tremula p. 13

Forget-me-not, Myosotis p. 15

Tormentill, Potentilla erecta p. 25

Narrow-leaved Bellflower, Campanula persicifolia p. 41

Sorbus hybrida (no English name) p. 54

Wood anemone, Anemone nemorosa p. 68

Bird-Cherry, Prunus padus p. 70

Birdsfoot-trefoil, Lotus corniculatus p. 79

Dandelion, Taraxacum p. 84

Dwarf birch, Betula nana p. 87

Mountain anemone p. 95

Glacier Crowfoot, Ranunculus glacialis p. 98

Scots Pine, Pinus sylvestris p. 111

Mountain Azalea, Loiseleuria procumbens p. 119